Contents

Introduction 2

How Effective Is Email Marketing Today? 4

Ways to use email marketing in your business 6

A Quick Word about Privacy 10

Four Key Products to Offer 11

The Definition of a Marketing Campaign 13

Different Types of Marketing Campaigns 15

The Four Step Lead Generation Process 18

Some quick tips on content writing 21

Deciding on an email marketing platform to use 23

A quick look at some jargon 25

Setting Up an Effective Email Campaign 28

Automation: A Marketers dream come true 48

How to Set Up Automation 51

Additional Email Marketing Tips 59

Perfect Email Marketing Recap 65

Thanks! (And next steps) 67

Bonus Offers 68

Tools 69

Introduction

A big thanks for choosing this book as your guide to getting better results with your email marketing.

Maybe you have never done email marketing before, or you send out emails to prospects regularly, but want to get better results? Either way, this book is for you.

In this book, I will demonstrate how you can generate more sales and grow your business using proven email marketing techniques. I will cover various elements including how to avoid spam folders, how to create subject lines that get emails opened and how to create content that entices customers to take actions such as buying from you.

I will also cover advice on how to create automated marketing campaigns and will suggest a range of apps that can help make life easier, without it costing you a fortune.

When working with many of my customers, I adopt a 4-step proven lead generation process which is highly effective at generating leads and converting them into sales. I will also go through this so that you can use the process as part of your marketing to generate more leads and grow your sales.

Many people are skeptical about the effectiveness of email marketing, or they aren't sure how to be effective and find it takes too much time and effort for too small a return, but I have included some facts and statistics that demonstrate how effective email marketing is. I will also demonstrate ways to get better results, often by keeping it simple.

Email marketing done badly can be ineffective and risk taking too much time to manage, but there is a solution. Email marketing automation not only saves time but can yield even greater results. We will discuss the benefits and different types of automation as well as go through a step-by-step guide to setting it up.

As a thank you for purchasing this book, I have included some special offers and bonus materials including email templates that you can use in your campaigns. These can be found later in the book.

My Approach to Email Marketing

I have over 25 years' experience in marketing, working in global businesses as well as supporting businesses to make sure they grow their sales through email marketing, social media and other online activities.

My proven approach to getting results is to use email marketing as part of a marketing strategy rather than on its own. Just sending out a few emails here and there won't bring you the results you want, and it can actually have negative consequences.

My 4-step lead generation process is guaranteed to bring results, and you will see in this book how it can ensure a steady stream of leads that are converted into customers.

There's a lot to cover! But before we get into the details of using email marketing, let's briefly discuss how effective email marketing is (just in case I haven't convinced you already...).

How Effective Is Email Marketing Today?

With the rise of social media, it's easy to get sucked into the belief that email marketing is a thing of the past, but this couldn't be farther than the truth.

According to Campaign Monitor (an email marketing platform) research shows a return on investment (ROI) for email marketing of 3800%.

That's an incredible statistic and not something to just glance over quickly, so let's just ponder this for a second. For every $1 you spend on email marketing, the report showed a return of $38.

Obviously, nobody spends just $1 on marketing so let's assume a business spends $1,000 on email marketing.

Would you invest that much if you could get a return of $38,000? I think that's what we might refer to as a no-brainer!

The report also showed this was an increase from an ROI of just under 2500% in 2013 so the trend is upwards in terms of how effective email marketing is. Even if this growth flattens out in the future, it's still a great return.

Other analysis also highlights how effective email marketing is and how it continues to be highly effective.

Here are some interesting facts according to Optinmonster in their 2021 article '40+ Email Marketing Statistics You Need to Know for 2021'[1]:

- 18% of companies achieve ROI greater than $70 per $1 invested.
- Email is 40x more effective at acquiring customers than Facebook and Twitter combined.
- Shoppers spend 138% more when marketed through email, as compared to those who do not receive email offers.

---

[1] Source: https://optinmonster.com/email-marketing-statistics/

Every day, we can receive updates and messages from a number of platforms including Facebook, Twitter, LinkedIn, WhatsApp and SMS text messages but over 99% of email users check their emails every day – and not just once, but as many as 20 times a day, according to Optinmonster.

It's even the first thing most people check at the start of the day with 58% checking email while on 14% check their social media updates!

If you are the kind of person that loves stats and you still remain unconvinced, then I recommend reading the Optinmonster article which can be found at the link below:

https://optinmonster.com/email-marketing-statistics/

Facebook may have hit 2 billion users worldwide in 2017 but the fact still remains that emails will remain core to the way we run our lives on a daily basis.

Even social media platforms rely on emails. To have a Facebook, LinkedIn or Twitter account you need to have a registered email address and they send you updates via email to make sure you don't miss anything on their platform.

A competitor and good friend of mine (yes, you read that right, we actually work together on opportunities as well) once sent out an email to his target audience pointing out the above fact. His argument was that if social media was so effective, why does Facebook need to email you updates. A good point.

The work environment also depends on email as a key method of communication and with very few exceptions, anyone making a booking or purchase online needs an email address to place their order and to receive order details.

Having an email address may not be as trendy or exciting as posting fun images on Instagram or having friends and family clicking to Like your posts on Facebook, but email will remain an important part of our online life for many years to come.

We aren't saying that other methods of online marketing should be ignored. In fact, it's the opposite.

As you will see later in this book, tools such as Facebook advertising and Google Ads should be used in conjunction with email marketing to attract and convert potential customers.

Email may not be the trendiest, but it's importance to the general public and to marketers remains as high as ever.

Ways to use email marketing in your business

There are various ways you can use email marketing in your business. While traditional and formal monthly newsletters aren't the most effective way to win new business (more on that later), they are one way to stay in touch with your target audience.

Other ways to use email marketing include fully automated lead generation processes with emails being sent in a 'drip' process over many days or weeks as well as one-off emails to prospects, which can also be followed up by further emails to let potential customers know that an offer you are promoting, for example, is coming to an end soon.

We will talk more about lead generation processes later but first, let's be clear on the pros and cons of one-off emails to potential prospects.

A single email to someone who doesn't know typically know your brand very well yields a low response rate. Sure, there are clever ways to prompt the reader to open the email and respond, such as by including an attractive subject and by using cleverly written wording but, if they don't know who you are then trust is low, and the reader is unlikely to buy from someone they don't know and don't trust.

Emailing people who don't know you also has legal implications as it impacts the privacy of the individual (see next chapter 'A quick word about privacy').

A single email, however, can be effective if used with other forms of sales and marketing. You might not be a great fan of cold calling, but I've seen a highly effective telemarketing campaign in the past where only the people who opened an email and clicked on a link were contacted in the first round of calls.

This assumes that the reader has enough of an interest in the services of the company to want to open the email AND click on a link in the email to find out more.

I have also seen one-off emails combined with interactions on social media to help build trust and awareness. It's also quicker and easier to send out a campaign with one, or at the most, two emails without having to design a sequence of emails and landing pages.

More than one email is always best

When it comes to the most effective use of email marketing, it's best to adopt the following two principles:

1. Using email as part of a wider campaign will get better results
2. More than one email is best and will increase sales

Whether you are hosting a webinar, running a training session, hosting a give-away competition, launching a new product or something else, the event will be more effective if email marketing is used as part of the campaign.

Sending out emails before and after the event will increase the chances of people attending, and it will also increase the chances of an attendee buying from you.

In fact, even if they don't attend, follow up email to none-attendees can still generate sales!

On the next page is a cut and paste from an email I received[2] which highlights how email marketing is crucial when used as part of a wider campaign – and a series of emails are sent out.

---

[2] Email received 31 Jan 2021 from Bryan at GrowthTools.com

Email Subject: *This email sequence = 68% of our sales*
From: Bryan @ Growth Tools

Email Content:

A couple years back, I noticed something pretty crazy about our sales numbers...

Every time we ran a webinar, **68% of our sales** *wouldn't occur until a day or two AFTER the webinar was over.*

Even more surprising? The majority of those sales came from people who watched **less than 20% of the webinar.**

That's the power of having a great sales email sequence.

Whether you're hosting webinars to sell your products or simply promoting them with email campaigns, you can dramatically increase sales by simply reminding people to buy at the right times...

There are some incredible facts in this email, and in case you are thinking that this is an isolated incident, it isn't. The reason Bryan gets these results is because he is following proven marketing concepts – techniques and processes which we know get better results, and which we will briefly discuss now.

Regular contact over time increases the chances of buying, as the customer begins to trust and become familiar with your brand. And smart campaigns that combine channels such as webinars and email marketing with content that add value is a foundation for successful marketing.

Imagine you get an email for a webinar you are interested in, and the content is of interest. You might not be ready to buy from the business hosting the event, but you sign up for the webinar.

Already you are starting to have more trust in the brand, but you still aren't ready to buy.

You join the webinar when it's live, but with a busy schedule and other pressures you have to jump off the webinar early. You still aren't ready to buy from them, but you can see that they know what they are talking about and how what they offer might help you.

Unfortunately for you, and the host, you miss the end bit which – as always – has the special offer and the call to action. But that doesn't mean it's the end and the lead generation process is finished.

After the event you receive a follow up email with details of the offer you missed on the webinar… an offer which you find interesting and decide to have a think about. With a busy schedule, you don't want to think about it too much right now but a couple of days later, you get a reminder email to let you know that the special offer ends in less than 6 hours.

It's FOMO time! (or fear of missing out). By now you know enough about who is offering the product or service and you know enough about the offer – and you like what they do (maybe you weren't too sure to begin with). It would be silly to miss this great offer.

This is just an example, and everyone reacts differently, but you can see how the follow-up sequence of emails can convert a potential prospect! A campaign like this will also still convert people who didn't attend the event.

In summary, don't just send one email out and think – or expect – it to be a great success. A sequence of well thought out emails that are used as part of a main campaign such as a webinar or product launch is one of the best ways to get results in marketing.

A Quick Word about Privacy

Over the past 20 or so years, privacy has increasingly become a hot topic. Nobody wants endless emails, phone calls and other content from spammers (I still don't know anything about that car accident I keep being told over the phone that I have been in…).

To protect our privacy, laws and regulations such as GDPR have come into force. Make sure when doing any email marketing that you are conforming to the laws of the region that you are operating in. The safest way to do this is to only send emails to people who have signed up or agreed to accept emails from you.

Email marketing platforms such as MailChimp and Constant Contact have tailored their software to make sure that you comply and that the emails you send out are GDPR compliant. You can, however, go beyond just complying with the law.

Businesses of the future should be ethical and treating someone's privacy with the highest level of respect and care it deserves is the best way to do this. You might want to be highly ethical because it's the right thing to do. It also has long-term benefits for the growth of your business.

Customers want to buy from companies that they trust. An example of this is with website lead generation. If your website has a sign-up form to add them to your email list, then they are more likely to sign up and stay subscribed if you make it clear that you will not share their information with anyone else.

According to HubSpot, addressing customer fears, like email spam or personal data use on a landing page with email capture, increases conversion rates by as much as 80%[3]!

The safer a potential customer feels and the more they trust you, the more likely they are to buy from you.

---

[3] For more information, go to https://jo.my/landing-page-stats

Four Key Products to Offer

Later, in the chapter 'the 4-step lead generation process', I will explain how to set up a lead generation process that involves email marketing. This proven process is highly effective in generating leads and converting leads in to paying customers. It does, however, require work and effort which I will also discuss.

First, I would like to introduce you to the concept of the 4 key products every business should offer in order to be a success. We can then understand how these key products relate to a lead generation process.

Every business should offer the following:

1. A Gift
2. A Lead Generation Product
3. Core Product
4. An Upsell Product

The **Gift** is a product that is offered for free with no strings attached. The person interested does not have to give up their email address, name or any bank account details. This product or service is used to build awareness of your brand, create trust and demonstrate you know your stuff!

An example of a Gift might be top tips and advice on a YouTube channel or information on your blogs. In both of these instances, someone can read or watch your content without having to commit to 'sign up' to anything.

A business won't make money directly by offering Gifts, but they are a critical part of long-term sales and are a great way to target the buyer who isn't ready to make a commitment of any sort - including giving away their email address.

A **Lead Generation Product** is one that requires a potential customer to give away some details, typically an email address. This information is then used as part of the lead generation and conversion process.

An example of a Lead Generation Product is a free whitepaper or eBook which is available on a landing page or is emailed once a potential customer enters their email address. We will go through this in more detail later when we talk about automation and the 4-step lead generation process.

Email marketing is usually a critical part of the process for offering a Lead Generation Product.

The **Core Product** is what you make money on (and if you don't then it may be time for a rethink of your business model!). When customers talk about your brand and your company, they should be familiar with your Core Product which could consist of several offerings.

The **Upsell Product** is something you make money on, but it isn't your Core Product. Many businesses have higher profit margins on Upsell Products than Core Products. The Upsell Product is something which existing customers may not be aware that you offer, or that new customers about to buy your Core Product might be offered during the transaction process.

Let's look at an example of how a company might offer all 4 product types…

A bike shop may offer videos on YouTube with advice for maintaining and riding a bike (it's Gift Product). They may also offer a free eBook via email on how to choose the right bike to suit your lifestyle (it's Lead Generation Product) and their store will be full of different bikes in different sizes and styles (its Core Product). The store will also offer Upsell Products such as an extended warranty, a service plan and a range of bike accessories.

Email marketing plays an important role, not just in offering the Lead Generation Product, but in promoting the Core Product and Upsell Products as well.

According to Alex Goldfayn in his book 'The Revenue Growth Habit', most customers only know about 25% of the services a company offers. That's an amazing statistic and shows how great the opportunity is to promote product offerings to people who are already customers of your business.

Using email marketing, you can promote the other 75% of services that you offer - increasing your sales and supporting existing customers in a way that makes them loyal advocates of your brand.

Here is a short list of how email marketing can play a role in promoting the four different products you sell:

> To capture email addresses and convert prospects when delivering the Lead Capture Product
> To create awareness of new Core Products when they are launched
> To promote existing Core Products that customers may not be aware of or have not considered buying in the past
> To remind or let customers know about Upsell Products straight after they have made their initial purchase
> To encourage repeat business over time. If a customer only needs your product or service every 3 or more months, then email marketing acts as a great reminder that you are there to help them out and to entice them back every 3 months

These examples, along with many more, show how email marketing can play its role as part of an overall marketing campaign.

Now we have discussed the different product types, let's understand the definition of a campaign and the different types of campaigns available so that you can see what's right for your business.

The Definition of a Marketing Campaign

So, what exactly is a Campaign? According to Google search, there are two definitions:

1. *a series of military operations intended to achieve a goal, confined to a particular area, or involving a specified type of fighting.*
2. *work in an organized and active way towards a goal.*

Source: Google Search

Clearly for most marketers (not involved in selling military equipment!) the second definition is the closest definition of a marketing campaign. Importantly, both definitions mention something that many marketers miss off when doing a marketing campaign.

Both definitions talk about a goal. It's important to be clear from the start when running a campaign what the goal is, and to focus activities around achieving that goal.

A business wanting to promote its eCommerce products for Prime Day (by Amazon) might run a short time-based campaign to sell as much as possible on Prime Day.

They may set a revenue target and the campaign could consist of email marketing, social media and other activities focused on directing people to their products on Amazon.

The example bike shop mentioned earlier is an example of a business running a long-term campaign with a goal to convert people downloading their free eBook to customers purchasing their Core Product.

In summary, a marketing campaign is a set of activities such as email marketing and social media advertising intended to achieve a goal. The goal might be a sales target, or it could be wider such as to achieve a level of brand awareness or launch a brand in a new market or country.

When it comes to email marketing, and in my opinion, there is a slight conflict in the definition of a campaign since most email marketing platforms refer to a campaign as one or more emails, and to a large extent ignore the use of other activities.

If you create a regular weekly email for example, then each email might be set up as a separate campaign when in fact in marketing terms, it's actually a single ongoing campaign.

This is nothing to worry about at this stage, but it's worth understanding as we will refer to campaigns through this book as both the wider term of marketing campaigns and as setting up an email campaign using email marketing software.

Different Types of Marketing Campaigns

Email marketing can be used in many different circumstances to generate sales. When I say, 'can be', I really mean 'should be'. By using email marketing in various different ways to reach your target audience at different times and in different circumstances, you are more likely to generate more sales.

Take an eCommerce business that offers fashionable clothing as an example. They might send out an email to someone who added an item to their shopping cart but didn't complete their order, to remind them that they have added items and that they are one click away from ordering.

The message and content of the email would be completely different to the potential customer who has signed up for the free eBook on how to find the right clothes for summer, or the campaign they send out to let customers know about an exciting new range of products that have just been launched.

Here are some examples of possible campaigns using email marketing to consider for your business:

Shopping cart abandonment: A series of emails to direct a potential buyer back to your site to finish off the order they started.

This could include reminders of the benefits you offer, a warning that stock is limited, and they will miss out if they leave it too long or a coupon with money off if they complete their order in the next 24 hours.

This campaign targets people who have a clear interest in your products and your brand but for whatever reason they have decided not to go ahead and place an order.

Lead generation: We have talked about this already. A potential customer lands on your website, enters their email address to receive something of value to them and email marketing is used to nudge the customer towards making a purchase.

Teaser campaign: This is to cause intrigue or get people to pre-register for something. An example might be that if you register your interest in a product then you will receive an exclusive offer or discount. The teaser campaign is effective when combined with other campaigns such as the Event campaign (see below).

One off promotion: This campaign includes a strong call to action to make a purchase. The offer should be for a limited time and is a one-off campaign such as over the summer or the festive period.

Examples include a 48-hour sale where users enter their email address to receive a 50% off code, or existing customers receive an email offering 20% off your upgrade services for 5 days only.

Event specific: This is similar to a one-off promotion but is focused on the goal of achieving registration or attendance to an event. It could be to attend a training you provide or to visit your stand at an exhibition.

This type of campaign works well with a teaser campaign which allows you to create more interest and secure more bookings early on.

Regular updates: This is what is commonly known as the Newsletter (although I'm not a great fan of this terminology. See later in the book why). Regular updates offer value to someone who has signed up to receive emails on a frequent basis. The content is varied, but always providing information that the reader wants to see and that is of great value to them.

Blog email: The blog email is a form of regular update, and it's a great way to keep customers informed, to drive visitors to your website AND to get better results from writing blog posts. A blog email simply contains the latest blog post that you have posted on your website.

To increase visitors to your website, it's best to not include the full blog post. Once the recipient has read what they can in the email, they should be left wanting to click on the 'more' button or link that takes them to the website to read the rest.

SendFox (www.sendfox.com) has a great feature called Smart Campaigns. It can be set up so that when you add a blog post to your website, SendFox will create an email with the content from your website. All you need to do is check over it and schedule the email to go out.

If you want to know more about blog writing to increase sales, then my book **Blogging for Business** on Amazon is also worth reading.

These are the main types of campaigns and it's possible to run different ones in parallel, or to merge campaigns so that customers who receive regular updates, for example, are also updated on one-off promotions and event specific campaigns if this adds value to them.

Note: Be very careful when merging campaigns. It's important that the recipient has signed up to receive this information. Just because someone has provided their information to receive information on an event, doesn't necessarily mean that they have agreed to receive regular updates. This can be considered spam and can potentially have legal consequences.

The Four Step Lead Generation Process

In this section I will focus on the Lead Generation product and outline a proven 4 step process for generating leads. The use of this process can apply to anyone selling to business customers as well as consumers and can also be used for eCommerce businesses.

The process uses four key ingredients:

The promotional trigger
The landing page
The Lead Generation Product
The email marketing campaign

The promotional trigger is used to reach out to your target audience and drive them to your landing page. It will include a call to action, offering your Lead Generation Product.

The promotional trigger could be a Facebook Ads campaign offering a free eBook as the **Lead Generation Product**.

When the advert is clicked, it will take the prospect to the **landing page** where they enter their email address in exchange for the eBook. Once this is done, an automated **email marketing campaign** starts with an initial email including the link to the eBook.

The email marketing campaign will then move the prospect towards making a purchase of the Core Product and possibly Upsell Products as well.

Using a personal fitness trainer as an example, the process and key ingredients would look something like this:

The promotional trigger:
A Facebook Ads campaign offering a free guide to healthy eating. Targeting people on Facebook who live nearby and have expressed an interest in fitness.

The landing page:
Purely focused on getting the visitor to enter their email address to receive their free guide.

The Lead Generation Product:
The free guide is delivered via email once the customer has entered their email address

The email marketing campaign:
Starts with an email containing the link to the free guide, followed by a series of emails providing top tips on getting fit and eating well. The emails will contain offers such as a free initial chat with the personal trainer or coupons to get 4 sessions for the price of 3.

It's important during the email marketing phase to offer valuable and relevant content. This will keep them subscribed and warmed up to the idea of receiving your emails that they want to read.

The offers should vary since everyone is different and one particular offer is not going to be for everybody.

The 4 sessions for the price of 3 idea mentioned earlier might be a bit too much for some people who aren't yet ready to commit to 4 sessions, but a free initial chat or 20% off your first session might be perfect for them.

The four-step lead generation process is proven to get results. The different ingredients will vary depending on the type of business you are in.

The promotional trigger could, for example, be a Google Ads campaign for people searching for what you offer, or it could be a LinkedIn Ads campaign to business owners. It could even be an email campaign from another source!

The whole process is focused around finding a new customer, reaching out to them and capturing their email address so that you can continue to market to them in a way that generates sales.

The Lead Generation Product that you offer MUST be strongly related to what you offer as your Core Product. There is no point offering something like free Amazon vouchers as this will generate interest from people who are not interested in your product or service at all.

If you are a florist, offer a guide on buying or looking after flowers. If you are an estate agent or realtor then offer a guide to buying the right house. I wouldn't download a guide to buying flowers or houses unless I had an active interest in buying flowers or a house.

Done this way, you know that the emails sign-ups are at least from prospects who have an interest in what you offer. Someone who does have an interest in flowers, or a house purchase is highly like to provide their email address in exchange for some valuable tips to help them with their purchase.

Now we have covered the main products and how they can be used in an effective marketing process, let's discuss how to create email campaigns that get results!

In the next chapter we will go through how to set up an effective email marketing campaign using an email marketing platform.

We will also include some important tips for making sure that the campaign is really effective. Afterall, it's pointless spending time putting together a campaign when nobody opens, read or acts on your emails!

Some quick tips on content writing

We will discuss how important effective content writing is in more detail later but it's worth pointing out that there are various apps you might want to consider for creating lead generation content.

Attract.io (visit https://attract.io) is a great tool for creating a lead magnet such as a free eBook, checklist or 'how to' guide. At the moment, this platform is completely free and has some amazing templates.

It has limitations such as the number of pages you can have, and the design isn't flexible, but there are two great things I love about Attrac.io.

Firstly, the templates look great and better than anything I have managed to create using Word or any other platform.

Even better still, a free guide can be created much quicker with Attract.io compared to messing around with other platforms. Oh, and did I mention that it's free?

The other great feature with Attract.io is that it hosts the lead magnet for you as an PDF. A common issue with creating a lead generation process is deciding where to host the product.

Google Drive, Microsoft OneDrive and Dropbox are other alternatives.

Another alternative to Attract.io for creating an eBook is Beacon (www.beacon.by). This is a more powerful solution but much harder to use and can take up a lot more time. At least, that's my experience.

When it comes to creating email content, also consider DripScripts which I discuss later.

Finally, we all make mistakes when writing content and it's important to review what's written.

Personally, I'm hooked on using Grammarly (https://app.grammarly.com).

This app doesn't just underline spelling mistakes, it also highlights text when the wrong grammar is used or a comma, question mark or full stop should be included.

It's easy to say its when it should be it's… you get the idea!

Grammarly also checks wording in emails and can be used in most browsers as well as apps such as Microsoft Word and Google Docs. You might want to pay for the premium solution, but the free version is good enough.

Deciding on an email marketing platform to use

There are various email marketing platforms available to use, but they all have similar functionality and use pretty much the same terminology such as 'lists', 'campaigns' and 'automation'.

If you are looking for a low-cost solution, then consider MailChimp or Moosend. Both of these offer some great basic functionality on the free plan and the links for both platforms are below:

https://mailchimp.com/
https://moosend.com/

Historically, I have been a great advocate of MailChimp which is free for as long as you have less than 2,000 subscribers, and it has been relatively easy to use. Unfortunately, the app has become a bit clunkier to navigate as it has expanded to offer other services such as for hosting websites and managing ads campaigns.

Another, bigger issue, is that the automation functionality is no longer on their free plan. This means that if you want to create a lead generation process that involves sending out more than one email automatically to a prospect then a monthly fee is needed.

While Moosend currently provides automation on its free plan, the platform isn't as powerful as MailChimp.

Another option for keeping the costs down is SendFox by AppSumo. I use this app which does everything you need, all for a one-off fee of $49!

You can find out more about SendFox here:

https://sendfox.com/

Or, if you are feeling generous, I earn a small amount of credit to spend on new apps if you sign up using this link:

http://fbuy.me/v/darrenhignett_2

There are plenty of higher-end solutions that cost a lot more money. Many of them offer features such as hosting landing pages and in fact, some of them are more focused on landing pages than email marketing.

Below is a list of some platforms to consider. Out of all of these, the top two I would recommend are HubSpot, because it has other solutions such as a CRM for tracking opportunities, and Keap, by Infusionsoft.

Keap is highly rated because of its high open rates and if you want as many people as possible to open your emails and to buy from you then Keap is recommend.

https://keap.com/
https://www.hubspot.com/marketing/free/f160
https://www.constantcontact.com/
https://www.activecampaign.com/
https://kajabi.com/features/email
https://www.clickfunnels.com/

Click funnels (the last link in the list above) is more focused on landing pages but has email marketing integrated.

A quick look at some jargon

Email marketing has some unique words which are fairly easy to understand. But let's cover them really quick now to avoid any confusion later on...

Lists:
Also known as an Audience. A list contains a compilation of email addresses. It will also likely contain additional information if this has been provided such as first name, last name and company name or telephone number.

You can have several lists such as a list for people who have signed up for the Lead Generation Product offer and a list for people who have signed up to receive regular updates. When creating an email campaign or automation, you will need to select a list to send the emails to.

If you are only just getting started with email marketing, then you are unlikely to have anybody in your list. That's natural and nothing to worry about at this stage. We will go through ways to grow your list later on.

Segmented Lists: This is a filtering of an existing list. Most email marketing platforms allow you to segment a list for a campaign. You may want to only send an email to people in the list who have signed up recently, or who have opened the last email as a follow up. Most platforms allow you to segment a list and then use this for sending out emails.

Some platforms allow you to split up your list by using 'tags' or 'labels' rather than segmented lists. In a way, it's similar but the main difference is that you can have multiple tags and the concept is easier to understand when creating email flows.

For example, imagine you are sending a series of emails to potential prospects about a series of events you are hosting.

If someone signs up for or attends one of the events in January, you might want to apply the 'attended January event' tag. The email flow could then be adjusted so that anyone who has that tag applied to them will receive a different set of emails, possibly thanking them for attending and letting them know about other events that they might also be interested in.

The difference in the message might be subtle but it can put off email subscribers if they get emails with messages such as 'we hope you enjoyed the event' when they didn't go, or 'why not come along to one of our events' when they have already been to a few of them.

Templates: Email software offers various pre-designed templates for you to write your email as well as the ability to create your own template from scratch. These templates allow you to quickly format the email to suit the content you want to send out - whether that's a template with 2 columns, 3 columns or just a regular plain template with a single column. When creating an email, you will be asked to select a template before writing the content.

For optimal delivery of emails, a simple or text-only template is best, although these templates don't look as snazzy or professional from a brand perspective.

Campaigns: A campaign in an email application will consist of a written email created from a template. It will also require a list or segmented list to be selected before sending the email. If that made sense, then we are starting to be clear on the different terms!

The steps to create a campaign will typically be as follows:

1. Create a list first
2. Create a new campaign
3. Enter email details such as subject header for the campaign
4. Select a template for the design of the email
5. Create the email by adding text, images, links etc
6. Select the List to send the email to
7. Send a test email to yourself and check the email is ready to go
8. Send the campaign to the list

The order of events may vary depending on what platform you use. Make sure to give relevant and descriptive names for your lists and campaigns. Once you start to create multiple lists and campaigns then you can easily get confused and it risks adding the wrong list of people to a campaign or automated flow.

Automation/Flows:

An automation campaign consists of a sequence of emails and other events. It might look something like this:

1. Send out initial email to new subscriber
2. Wait 48 hours
3. Send follow up email
4. Wait 5 days
5. Send email #3
6. ... and so on

Automations can be much more complex than this by using tags. It can include steps such as, if the subscriber has the ABC tag applied then follow this sequence. Otherwise, follow this flow sequence.

Automations are also called flows in some apps. In Mailchimp when you click on Automations, it then refers to the various automations as Customer Journeys. I like the idea of this.

When you set up a flow or automation, you are taking the customer on a journey which could be from signing up to receive an eBook through to learning about your products and then becoming a customer.

Whether it's journeys, flows, automation or something else, this kind of automation is very powerful and can save a lot of hours managing your marketing. We will talk more about these automation flows later on.

Setting Up an Effective Email Campaign

In this section we will focus on the set up of a manual campaign, including the critical factors for success. We will cover the setup of automation later on, but the fundamentals of a successful campaign covered here apply to automated campaigns as well.

If you don't have an account with an email software platform, head over to one of the links in the last section and register an account (oh, and it won't surprise you that you will need an email address to sign up!).

To make an email incredibly effective, follow these rules:

Create a subject line with one objective: To get the email opened!

Despite the strong ROI of email marketing the open rate on emails worldwide is low, but your subject line is an opportunity to change that.

According to OptinMonster, the average open rate of emails in Q2 of 2016 was 25%. From experience, I've seen open rates as high as 35-40% as well as clients requesting help due to open rates being as low as 5%!

The fact that around 3 in 4 people don't open up emails from a campaign doesn't look good, but an open rate above 20% is typical.

There are many reasons why emails don't get opened. Some emails go straight to spam, never to be seen by the intended recipient (more on that later). Some people are simply so busy that they don't see the email in their inbox or at least, on a conscious level, they might not notice it as they are distracted by other emails just above or below your email in their long list of unopened emails.

Other people see the email you have sent but decide to ignore it or delete it. This is the area we will focus on here. How to entice the reader to open your email.

So... how do we increase open rate on emails that appear in the inbox?

The key to success is in the subject line. The subject content MUST catch their attention AND make them want to open the email immediately. There are two objectives here. Grab their attention AND make them want to open the email. Even having them think "That might be interesting, but I'll take a look at it later" is most likely going to lead to them to NOT opening the email.

Take the following examples:

Imagine you are under pressure to get a home or work task done, and you see the following subject lines.

Would you open any of these emails based on these 3 subject lines?

April Newsletter
A general update from ABC Inc.
<BLANK>... no subject line!

The above headlines are unlikely to attract you to opening them. The fact that the subject line has not been filled in might sound like an exaggeration but, it does happen, and it will put off a lot of people from opening the email if it isn't from a highly trusted and known source.

Some stats to consider

The challenge with the subject line is to increase the open rate. You aren't going to be able to get every person in a large list of email recipients to open the email but, if you send out a campaign to 1,000 email subscribers, then an increased open rate from 20 to 30% means an extra 100 people reading your emails, and one way to achieve this is – as you know by now – with an appealing subject line.

I have often raised an interesting question in discussions with business owners and marketers. Should you spend more time on the subject line than on the content in the email? And is the subject line, effectively more important than the content itself since great content is wasted if the email isn't opened up?

Whether or not it's more important, it certainly requires more thought and effort than simply spending 2 minutes quickly fudging a subject line such as 'November Newsletter' or 'Update on our team' so that you can get on with the content and sending out the email. A subject line like this is about as boring and unexciting as it can get!

It's important to remember that we all lead busy lives, and our email inbox gets full very quickly. Many people will quickly decide whether to open an email or not based on what the subject line says.

The title that includes the above examples with wording such as 'newsletter' don't give a reason to want to open it. The wording doesn't cause intrigue or desire to take further action. Even a loyal brand advocate who is busy might at best, archive the email or decide to read it later, but never get round to reading it.

Email subjects should be relevant to the content and should include what the great benefit is of opening the email. This could include sentences starting with 'how to', '7 ways to' or 'become/learn/grow'. Here are some examples for a business coach:

7 Ways to Delegate and Grow Your Business as a Result
Grow Your Business with these Great Tips!
Claim Your Free eBook And Discover How to Be A World-Class Manager

All of the above have a clear benefit (grow your business as a result, grow your business thanks to some great tips, a free eBook and be a world-class manager).

They also create some intrigue that will make you want to open the email. Wouldn't you like to know what those 7 ways are, or what those great tips are?

It has to be worth opening up the email from the last subject line mentioned above, just to see what the free eBook is! With all of these, I would at least open the email to quickly scan the contents and find out a bit more.

Once we have the reader's attention and they are going to open the email, it's critical to get the first few lines of the email to do their job. Before we do that, the preview area also plays an important role...

Tease with the preview area

The preview area appears in inboxes before an email is opened. It's designed (as the name suggests) to give the reader a preview of what the email is about.

How many times have you seen an email and the preview area says, 'Use this area to offer a short preview of your emails content'? You may not have noticed, but there was a time a few years ago when I used to see it frequently. It's the default wording provided by the software platform and it only takes a few minutes to change it, yet so many companies don't!

Even big brands forget to replace the wording with their own content and seeing this default wording tells me the email is about a badly written email campaign that I might not be interested in! At the back of my mind, I'm thinking this is a spam email, while I try to work out if it's worth opening.

The preview area is meant to build on your subject line (rather than look like you haven't put the effort in). Using the example above with the subject line '7 Ways to Delegate and Grow Your Business as a Result', a preview area might say 'Proven delegation tips from millionaire entrepreneur xx' or 'Delegation tips can could change your life - and your business'.

This reinforcement of the key message, and the benefit of opening the email increases the intrigue - and the desire to want to open the email.

Consider using Emojis 😊

Emojis – you either love them or you hate them (should I include a happy face and a sad face here?). Over the years, emojis have become more widely accepted for using in marketing. I remember having chats with customers in the past who felt that using emojis was reserved for teenagers and might come across as unprofessional, but opinions have shifted.

Using emojis in marketing brings life to content and allows a brand to come across as being more human – and the benefits of using emojis are backed up by research.

According to WordStream[4], emojis can increase engagement on Twitter by 25%, and shares on Facebook by 33% (as well as overall interactions by 57%). The research was a few years ago, but I'm confident that the importance and effectiveness of emojis has increased since then.

But what about email marketing, and subject lines?

I'm glad you asked 😊. According to a report by Experian[5], the majority of brands that used emojis in their subject lines experienced a higher open rate, while Campaign Monitor states in an article that *"Emojis in subject lines can lead to higher response rates than traditional email, meaning you could be missing an opportunity to engage your readers if you don't use emojis"*.

Inboxes are crowded with text-based subject lines. Having a single emoji in a subject line can make a big difference in standing out and enticing the recipient to open the email.

Other research backs this up further. According to Business Wire[6]:

"Around Valentine's Day, email subject lines including the "lips" emoji drove a read rate of 24 percent" … compared to 20 percent in text-only subject lines, while Father's Day emails with a wrench emoji in the subject line also increased open rates and read rates.

One caution to consider – I used the word 'consider' in my title for this section as emojis aren't the solution for all campaigns and businesses. It's probably not a great idea for a lawyer to send emails with emojis in the subject line, and using the wrong

---

[4] https://sproutsocial.com/insights/emoji-marketing/
[5] https://www.campaignmonitor.com/resources/guides/using-emojis-and-symbols-in-email-marketing/
[6] https://www.businesswire.com/news/home/20170523005359/en/Emojis-Increase-Read-Rate-Won%E2%80%99t-Automatically-Land

emojis or too many emojis can also backfire and negatively impact the image or credibility of the brand or the content of the email.

Emojis work best for consumer retail businesses and seasonal events, but they can risk reducing credibility for businesses selling to other businesses or for professional industries where the tone of the message in the email, and the subject line itself need to be more serious.

In summary, consider using emojis in your email marketing campaigns to increase open rates in emails, but make sure that the use of emojis is right for the context, the message and the audience you are targeting.

Avoid Spam folders with these tips

So far, we have talked about making subject lines and preview areas that are attractive and that 'just have to be opened' (no, no, I can't wait… I have got to see what this email says…), but what about the dreaded spam folder? If the email doesn't even arrive in the inbox, then the battle has been lost before the start.

Here are some tips for making sure your email campaign avoids the spam folder.

Reduce images

Images in emails are often seen by email clients as suggesting that an email is a newsletter. Email platforms such as Zoho automatically add emails with images to the 'Newsletter' folder (who reads these?), while other email hosting services send them directly to the spam folder. Plain text emails might not sound glamorous, but they increase the chances of being opened by managing to escape the spam folder.

Have a maximum of 3 links in your email

Having links that send readers to your landing page or eCommerce shop are great. They get results. But there is a tradeoff. While having links is good, having too many links means that your email is more likely to land in the spam folder.

Email clients have got smart at spotting spam, and an email with lots of links is one of the criteria (alongside having embedded images) that they use to redirect email to the spam folder.

According to Genoo[7], you should keep the number of links in an email to under five, although two to three links is optimal. They also state:

Keep the number of links in any email under five. Two or three is best. This includes any links on images or social links

And…

Focus your links on what will bring you the most value – don't link to tangential things that take people off-track. You'll lose them.

When it comes to the exact number that's acceptable, there are various figures I have seen by email marketing experts, but I suggest 3 as an absolute maximum. Remember – while having links in your email are important, they are useless if your email doesn't get opened!

Clean your list to reduce bounce backs

If an email client gets a lot of bounce backs (in other words, they can't be delivered to the recipient), then it uses this as a measure to assume that the email being sent is spam. When you send out a campaign, make sure to remove any email addresses that bounce back so that future email campaigns are more effective.

There might be a good reason why the email has not been delivered. A potential customer might be using a work email address, for example, but has left the company or someone signing up to your list entered the wrong email address. Whatever the reason, dormant and closed email accounts that are on your list are going to increase the chances of your campaign being too popular with the dreaded spam folder.

---

[7] https://genoo.com/links-in-emails-how-many-should-i-have/

Set up email authentication

Sorry, I'm about to get technical and a bit geeky.

Email authentication (also known as domain authentication) is about verifying that emails are sent from who they say they are coming from. Too many phishing and other scams nowadays are sent out claiming to be from official businesses such as banks. We have all received that email from a bank saying that we need to click here to reset our password when in fact it's a scam, right?

Email authentication is critical to ensuring that content is delivered to your mailing list. By authenticating your domain address, you are telling email clients that your domain is real.

According to Campaign Monitor[8]:

"As part of the email delivery process, receiving mail servers work to determine the authenticity and legitimacy of your email.

When a mail server receives your email, it basically asks, "Is this email from who it says it's from? How do I verify that? What do I do if the email is not successfully authenticated?"

Receiving mail servers will also look at the sending reputations associated with the sending domain and sending IP. Content, previous engagement for your sends among their users, and other reputational factors will also factor into whether your email will successfully get delivered to the intended inboxes."

Personally, I find the process of email authentication a bit of technical pain, despite considering myself to be somewhat technical for a marketer.

Even this week, while writing this, a customer emailed me excitedly to let me know the platform he is using has added email authentication, but after 2 days of chat

---

[8] See https://www.campaignmonitor.com/blog/email-marketing/2019/07/email-authentication-solving-mystery-authentication/

support and posting on Facebook Groups, he emailed me again saying "*Darren – you were right. This isn't as straightforward as I thought it would be*".

Privacy, passwords and security are absolutely necessary, if only there was an easier way!

To set up email authentication, each email platform should have instructions on how to do this. Without getting too geeky, you need to have the right SPF records and DKIM key that the receiving server can validate.

I recommend visiting the help section for the platform you are using (such as MailChimp, SendFox etc) and searching for "how do I authenticate emails". If you still can't find the answer, then use the keywords **SPF records** and **DKIM key** in your search.

If you are thinking "this sounds like a lot of effort. Is it worthwhile?", the answer is yes, it's worth sorting out. If you are serious about email marketing, then don't procrastinate and delay setting up email authentication. The longer you leave it, the more you will be losing out.

Create a heading with one objective: To make the reader want to read on!

So far you have tips and advice for avoiding the spam folder and for getting your emails opened. Now let's move on to the content in the email in more detail.

Once the email is opened, the first thing that will be visible will either be an image/logo, a headline or the first paragraph. Having an image or a headline is optional and in many circumstances isn't recommended (see later in this chapter).

If you are going to have a headline, then create it with a similar objective to the subject line - to make the reader want to read more. While the subject line creates a desire to want to open the email, the headline should make the reader want to read the first paragraph and the first paragraph should make the reader want to read the rest of the email!

Think of this concept as each stage having the objective of getting the reader to go to the next stage - from opening an email to reading the opening part then from reading the opening part to reading the main content and then to taking an action (such as clicking on a link).

Subject line: entice people to open the email
Headline: Create intrigue so that the first paragraph is read
First paragraph: Convince the reader to want to read the rest of the content
Main content: Cleverly convince the reader to want to click on the call to action

The headline could be similar to the preview area. It could clarify the subject further (such as by explaining what the eBook is in the example above), or it could tease with wording such as mentioning that the tips or eBook are guaranteed to make a difference in some way.

If you're not sure about a headline then leave it out - or if you are still keen to keep it then show it to colleagues and ask them 'would this really, really make you want to read on?'. If the answer is no, then either make changes, or remove the headline.

Don't 'bury the lead'. The first paragraph should capture the essence of the content

Burying the lead is an expression in journalism where the most exciting parts of an article that grab the reader's attention are buried further down in the article and therefore ineffective.

In journalism, burying the lead means less people buying the publication as the opening paragraph and headline aren't appealing. In email marketing it means people reading less of the content and not acting on the call to action.

If the key message or benefits of what you are offering is buried deep within your content, then it's wasted if the reader doesn't get past the first paragraph.

According to Uberflip, average website visitors only read 20% of the text on a page. Most people who read a web page or a campaign email skim rather than read a full article, and if the opening paragraph doesn't capture their attention then they will quickly turn their attention elsewhere… and won't read the rest of your email or take action by clicking on those links that you have beautifully crafted!

If your email starts by saying you have a free eBook, but you don't point out how it has benefited other people, or how it will make a massive difference to the reader until near the end of the email, they may never get to read these benefits and therefore, won't understand why they should access the eBook.

If the objective of your email campaign is to drive them to an eBook where they can understand more about your services, then wording such as 'Discover how to ABC in less than a week with this free eBook" will be much more effective than wording that simply says "I've launched a free eBook that you might be interested in. The book contains a wealth of information about…".

I don't know about you, but I was lost at "might be interested in.". On a busy day, I'm not going to scroll to the bottom to find out what why I should get the book.

However, if you include these benefits and other valuable information in the first paragraph in a way that they can relate to, then it's clear why a reader should continue to read on. Consider these two examples:

Example 1:

First paragraph:
Our team management skills event is taking place on October 10th. We've been planning it for a while, and we would love you to come along if possible. Below is more information.

Final paragraph:
This event will help you become better at team management. The course includes tips on how to handle conflict resolution and motivate team members to get better results.

Example 2:

First paragraph:
Learn how to motivate your team better, increase productivity and motivate staff with this short course that's proven to get results

The last paragraph isn't shown in the second example, as it's irrelevant to the point I want to make. The point here is that the second example is much more effective as the crucial benefits, and reason for the event (and reason to read on) are covered at the start.

In the first example, the opening paragraph explains there is a team skills event and when it is, but it doesn't convince anyone why they should attend or find out more. If it was from a person you know very well personally then the wording 'would love you to come along' might have an impact, but it's unlikely to be the case in a mass email marketing campaign.

The second example, however, clearly shows you will get a lot out of the course, and it's backed up by the fact that it's proven to get results. Now I want to know more! ...And now you can tell me more details such as when it is.

Another element of a great paragraph is intrigue. You may not be able to cover much in an opening paragraph, but if you can cause intrigue to make the reader want to carry on then they are more likely to stay with you.

Another great tip to consider when creating a headline, as well as for the subject line, is to finish on a strong word that the reader wants to act on. This doesn't always work but here are some examples:

Discover 7 ways to grow your business
Discover 7 ways to achieve business results

The last word that is read is more memorable. Finishing with the word 'results' is much more powerful than finishing with the word 'business'. Overall, both sentences might be good, but the last one might just improve your results.

Find out how to become fitter and healthier with this new app
Download this app if you want to become fitter and healthier

Like the first example, ending with the word 'healthier' or the phrase 'fitter and healthier' is better than 'app' or 'new app'.

Sometimes finishing with a stronger word or phrase means re-writing and re-ordering the words and the difference in the two examples is subtle but try to get into the habit of finishing strong with headlines and any wording in your marketing that is designed to stand out.

You MUST have a strong call to action

Not just a call to action, but a strong call to action!

Having an email that ends by saying 'reply to this email and let me know if you would like to attend the event' isn't strong. It's a call to action and it's a friendly way of writing, but there is no urgency, no clear benefit and it doesn't trigger anything in the reader's brain that says TAKE ACTION!

The response is more likely to be 'ok, I will do' followed by the reader putting the email to one side and carrying on with their everyday life.

A strong call to action should include the benefits such as 'if you would like to improve your team management skills then register now' or 'if you would like to become a more effective team manager…'.

Sentences like these get the reader thinking about their actions. Subconsciously they may ask themselves 'if I don't reply, does that mean I don't want to improve my team management skills or be a more effective team manager? Of course I do! Maybe I should take the course?'

If you are including a button, then the wording in the button should be kept short which means that you will need to position your wording on the benefits just above the button.

For example, you might write 'Register now using the button below and learn how to ...', followed by a button that takes the reader to your landing page.

It's important for a strong call to action to stand out and that's the great thing about buttons. We seem to have been somehow trained over the years to click on buttons. We just can't resist. Having a button as a call to action is much more likely to be clicked on than a bit of wording that has a hyperlink in it.

Later on, I will talk about using power words such as now, unique and limited, but it's worth including these in your call to action as well as a bit of scarcity.

If spaces are limited or the offer ends soon then there is a scarcity factor. There are only so many places or so much time, and the reader might not want to miss out.

If your offer is also unique and exclusive to email subscribers, then they will feel valued for being on your email list – and they will also want to take advantage of an offer that's in some way special.

Include links in your content. But be selective.

Email solutions such as MailChimp and Constant Contact allow you to include links in emails that are trackable. This has a huge benefit in terms of understanding how effective a campaign has been, as well as what happens after the initial email has gone out.

Links should also be part of your call to action. Using the event example above, a link may send the reader to a landing page to register for the event and make payment.

Amazon is a great example of a company that uses links clicked to generate emails. I've seen examples in the past whereby if you click on the Audiobooks section on a Kindle, you get an email offering a free trial. If you view laptops on Amazon, you get an email later on with suggested laptops that are available.

The same principle applies to links in an email campaign. It's possible to create more tailored content to recipients based on what links they click on within the email.

When creating links in emails you can create multiple links to test what the user likes. A digital marketer providing training and tips via email might include a link for tips on Twitter and another for tips for LinkedIn.

If a user clicks on the Twitter related link but not the LinkedIn one, then this is a sign that they have some interest in Twitter and want to know more about using Twitter for their business.

This information can then be used to target the reader with content around using Twitter, including more top tips for using Twitter and possibly a special offer for personalized training on how to use Twitter to grow sales.

When using multiple links, be careful. It's easy to have too many links that confuse the message of the email and give the reader too much choice. Research shows that when faced with too many options, customers tend to go for not making a decision. In email terms this translates into a reader not clicking on any links.

In my book, How To Create A Perfect Landing Page, I urge anyone creating a landing page to focus on just one call to action and to make the landing page as distraction free as possible. For email marketing the decision to use one or more links depends on the type of campaign.

A regular updates campaign is more likely to have multiple links as you pack more value into the emails, but an Event campaign is more likely to have one call to action - register now.

And don't forget to keep the total number of clicks to a maximum of 3 if you want to avoid landing in spam folders!

Use Power Words Throughout the campaign

If you have read any of my previous books or taken a Think Twice Marketing course you will be familiar with my passion for power words. These are words that make a difference in your marketing. They come in various flavors but essentially, they can make a huge difference to how a reader reacts and if they become a customer.

Below are some examples with the power word in bold - and an explanation in brackets:

*We sell **delicious** ice cream (it sounds so much more appealing than just we sell ice cream)*

*We help you develop a **successful** marketing strategy (do you want a marketing strategy or a successful marketing strategy?)*

*Call us **now** to find out more (the word now is proven to trigger an action in the brain to take action)*

*This offer is available for a **limited time** only and is **guaranteed** to bring results! (limited or limited time creates scarcity in the mind and people don't want to miss out. The word guaranteed gives confidence and holds much more power than just saying it will bring results).*

I would love to send out a list of over 100 power words you can use in your marketing.

To receive this for free (it's my gift!), just email me personally using the email address below and quote FREEPOWERWORDS. I will then send you a list of over 100 power words including more information and examples of how power words can make a difference to your marketing.

darren@thinktwicemarketing.com

So far, we have covered the key points to creating a successful email marketing campaign - from having a subject line with one objective through to using power words. If you follow these guidelines you will achieve much better results with more people opening your emails, more people reading the content and more people taking positive action.

The next time you sit down to write your email campaign, I recommend reading through these elements again to make sure your campaign is effective.

Now, let's discuss a few other points related to email marketing that will help improve results.

Classic newsletters don't work. Personal emails do work

Earlier on I mentioned that I don't like newsletters. Actually, the idea of sending regular emails with information that provide value is the right way to do email marketing, but the dislike is to do with the positioning and the way it's perceived by your target audience.

The problem is that a subject line that says 'newsletter' (or suggests in some way that it is a newsletter) along with the classic newsletter-style email with images, columns and talks about what's new at your company doesn't work.

The open rate on the classic style newsletter is much lower and even if readers open the email, they seldom take action or find it of high value. Campaign types discussed earlier and themed emails such as how to achieve something, how to delegate etc offer much higher value, get more interactions and achieve a higher open rate.

Try to avoid email content that follows this traditional newsletter-style and instead focus on the types of campaigns that we have talked about earlier in the book. These campaigns have a clear objective (such as to achieve sign up to an event) and are focused on something that the reader should find valuable.

Added to the perception, is the fact that newsletter-style emails are more likely to go to spam folders. Subject lines with the word 'newsletter', content with images and lots of links are factors we have already discussed that add up to journey destined to arrive in spam folders!

Emails that are personal also achieve greater results, and it's possible to personalize and include information such as the recipient's first name in a campaign email. I have experienced a much higher response rate to emails when it's written to represent a more personal one-to-one email, rather than a format that looks like a one-to-many mass email campaign.

Consider the following email that achieved a response rate 5 times higher than any emails sent previously over an 8-week period:

Hi John,

I hope business is good? Just a quick message to let you know that our next business networking event with over 20 businesses attending is this Friday at 8am.

Would you like me to book you in?

Regards,
Darren

This email contained no images (and yes - indeed, no links) but the very personal nature of the email achieved an incredible response rate!

People love content that's personal to them. The wording above was short, to the point and asked a question. Even if a business owner couldn't make it, they still responded which is highly unusual for many email campaigns we see today.

Images create an impression, good or bad

We are back to the discussion of images again, but this is the last time, I promise!

Attractive images on social media, websites and in brochures are attention grabbing and can dramatically improve results. In emails they can also improve the professional image of a brand, but there are a couple of problems with using images in email campaigns:

Firstly, images embedded in an email are more likely to get picked up by spam filters who will classify the email as spam.

Secondly, images can create an appearance of being more of a newsletter and less personal - the pros and cons of which we have already discussed.

Compare the above personal email to one you might receive with an image of the networking event, large call to action buttons, social media logos and the networking logo. It might come across as being very professional, but the personal email is appreciated more, and I can guarantee from experience, it will get better results.

That doesn't mean you shouldn't use images in your emails but take into consideration the possible impacts if you do.

Images can tell a story about your event or new product you are launching, but this must be weighed up against the benefits of being more personal or how many spam folders your email will arrive in.

How frequent should emails go out in a regular email campaign?

You will notice the title doesn't tell you the answer like the previous titles do. And that's because it depends!

Many marketers instinctively feel that it's best to not send emails out too often because we all hate how many emails we find in our inbox. But this can actually work against you.

It's all about familiarity...

Receiving emails once a month or less frequent than that is likely to result in a higher rate of people unsubscribing as they are not familiar with your emails, and who you are. They are less likely to see value in content that you send - even if it is of high value!

I'm sure you have received an email from a sender you don't know and, if the subject line doesn't look familiar, then you have unsubscribed. It could well have been from someone you subscribed to a year ago and they only send out an email every 5 or 6 months. There may be some value for you in the email, but you will never know as it gets swiftly moved to the trash folder.

Likewise, subscribers who receive regular emails from a known source and that add value are more likely to stay subscribed. They are also more likely to open emails and take action.

The question then, is, how often is too often?

If someone is new to receiving emails from you then it's better to send more frequent emails in the initial stages to increase familiarity and so that subscribers get used to receiving emails from you.

I have heard business owners baulk at the idea of sending emails every day, but the most effective email marketers do just that! They send emails every day or two days providing valuable information, mixed in with occasional bursts of promotional campaigns.

The frequency of emails also depends on the type of campaign and the dynamics of your own industry, including the people in your email list and their expectations.

If someone signs up to receive updates of an event launch, then they are more likely to expect a few emails when the event is not for a while followed by a burst of emails as the event launch gets nearer.

In this instance, 2 emails a day in the last few days before the event is considered acceptable as you provide them with the latest updates and reminders.

Automation: A Marketers dream come true

In this chapter, we will discuss automation marketing and how it can be used to benefit your business in a huge way. We will also go through how to set up an automated email marketing campaign.

Imagine sitting on a Caribbean beach sipping a cocktail as the sun goes down. While you sit there, a customer who added a product to their shopping cart on your website but abandoned it, gets an email offering them 10% off if they complete the order in the next 24 hours. They check back in and complete the order.

A visitor to your YouTube channel also visited your site and downloaded the free eBook. She has read it and is so impressed that they are just in the final stages of confirming their budget to spend with you. At the same time, another prospect who has received regular emails from you over the last 6 weeks is convinced by your latest email you have just sent them that they should buy from you.

This is great news! The sales and marketing process continues to work, and emails are being sent out without any manual interaction. It sounds too good to be true!

You might not be a fan of cocktails or sitting on beaches but that's ok. Email automation works whether you are in a meeting, travelling or anytime throughout the day. Even while you are sleeping.

Email automation involves setting up a process within the email marketing platform. It's a bit of work initially but once it's set up, it runs automatically and looks something like this:

Trigger: Receive a new email from the website
Action: Send out the introductory email (email number 1) to that recipient

Trigger: 2 days after receiving a new email from the website
Action: Send out email number 2

Trigger: 5 days after receiving a new email from the website
Action: Send out email number 3

The number of triggers and emails can depend on the campaign. You simply configure the trigger (such as how many days) and write the email associated to each trigger.

When an email platform receives a new subscriber then it sets off a trigger within the automation flow.

We will go through setting up automation in more detail later, but first, here are the benefits:

A standard, proven model you can repeat

Email automation is proven to bring results. Once you are happy with the flow of emails and the content then you can be sure it will continue to operate and bring results. Sometimes when doing it manually, it's easy to deviate from an effective process as different staff write emails differently, and processes can easily be forgotten. That doesn't happen with automation.

Immediate support for your prospect

If you are away or it's the weekend, then the emails still go out promptly. A potential customer who requests your free eBook on a Friday night doesn't want to wait until you finish your meeting on Monday morning to receive his copy via email. This delay will lose sales, especially if you have an online store and someone is wanting to place an order.

A quick response comes across as more professional, and shows you are serious about caring for the customer.

With eCommerce, customers will go elsewhere very quicky and while potential customers when selling business to business might be a bit more patient, the delays in receiving emails will increase the chances that they will buy from someone else who is prompter and is perceived to be more professional!

It's cost effective

Depending on how you set it up, there may be some integration costs or subscription fees, but there are many tools out there that are free and email automation is free with Moosend and SendFox.

Added to this, having a flow of emails going out to a number of people automatically is much lower cost than paying someone (or spending your own time) to send them out manually.

Less errors

Have you ever sent an email to the wrong person? Or re-read your email at a later date and spotted bad grammar or badly written wording? If you have, you're not alone! Automation avoids the risk of making mistakes like this.

Once you are happy with the automation process and the wording then the content will always be consistent, and the order and timing of the emails will always be delivered as you expect.

Less errors, including forgetting to send out a follow-up email means higher sales conversions!

How to Set Up Automation

With so many hosting platforms for websites, apps and email marketing platforms, it's difficult to give detailed instructions on how to set up an automation process and you may need to work with your web designer to get their advice on what's best to use.

The good news is that many platforms over the last few years have made it much easier to set up an automation. Various platforms combine landing page hosting with email automation to make the entire lead generation process so much easier and effective!

In this chapter, I will go through examples for setting up a lead generation process where you are promoting a lead generation product using the proven 4-step lead generation process mentioned earlier.

As a recap, this model involves your target audience visiting a landing page, entering their details and then receiving an email with a free eBook, checklist or something else that you are offering.

For this model, the following types of platforms are typically needed to create this process:

A website hosting platform (such as WordPress, Weebly, Wix) with a landing page
A form builder for creating a data capture/entry form
An email marketing platform (such as Constant Contact, MailChimp)

The form on the site is created using the form builder, which is also responsible for sending the email address and other details automatically to the email marketing platform. The email marketing platform then runs the automation process for sending out emails.

It may be that the hosting platform for your website has automation included or built-in, and it would make sense to use this rather than having to find other apps and platforms to use.

As I mentioned earlier, some platforms include website or landing page hosting along with email automation as well. I will go through these platforms in more detail later.

Assuming you aren't using an all-in-one platform, I'm going to go through two examples using a choice of tools and apps. The first will be using a WordPress site and the other is using Weebly to create a landing page. Both examples are focused on promoting a Lead Generation Product.

Once we have gone through the two examples, we will cover how to set up the automation campaign so that a sequence of emails is sent out over a period of time.

If you are outsourcing the setup of your process, then you might want to skip the next sections that discuss WordPress and Weebly.

WordPress Example

Using WordPress, there are many plug-ins to create forms or manage email marketing. I have used SumoMe in the past which allows you to create different types of forms such as a pop-up box with a call to action or what they refer to as a landing mat with a call to action and form to fill in.

SumoMe integrates with email platforms such as MailChimp, GetResponse and Mailgen (make sure to check what platforms integrate with each other before you set up an account as well as what the fees are for the different tools).

First of all, set up an account with your chosen email marketing platform and create a list, or audience. Then simply install the SumoMe plugin to your WordPress site, set up a SumoMe account and create your offer.

You then need to connect your SumoMe account to your email marketing platform. You will be asked which email list you would like email addresses to go to, so make sure you have an account set up with an email marketing platform and a list created before connecting SumoMe to your email software.

Once this is done, head over to your email marketing platform and create your automation process for sending out emails, which we will cover later.

A good alternative to SumoMe is JotForm. This neat app allows you to create your form with the color, wording and other formatting to suit you. You then cut and paste the code it gives you into your site and your form is built. You will then need to connect it to your email marketing platform, like with SumoMe.

Here are the links to the two apps:

www.jotform.com
www.sumo.com

To sum up, the process is as follows:

- Set up an account with an email marketing platform
- Create a list or audience that you want sign-ups to go to
- Install a form builder plug-in such as SumoMe in WordPress
- Create a page on your website with a form using the plug-in
- In the settings for the form, set the form submissions to go to your new list that you have set up in your email platform (for example, SumoMe settings so that data from completed forms go to your 'free eBook' list in MailChimp
- Now set up the automation in your email marketing platform

Weebly Example

If you are not familiar with Weebly, it's a great drag and drop website builder like Square Space and WiX that has its own email marketing platform and form builder built in. For sites that are a single landing page it's easy to use, and you can quickly make a great looking landing page.

Although Weebly has its own email marketing platform, it also integrates into other email marketing platforms. Using the Weebly email platform (called Weebly Promote) is the easiest option but I recommend using a third-party platform which has more functionality in terms of automation.

Once you have created your form in Weebly using the drag and drop functionality, either visit Weebly Promote to create your automation or connect a third-party email platform. To do this, visit the Apps store from the top menu.

Note: Always check what Weebly or other sites and forms integrate to in terms of email platforms first to avoid wasting time setting up landing pages or accounts to tools you can't use!

The process for using Weebly is similar to WordPress and should look like this:

- Install an email marketing app in Weebly and check with email platforms it integrates to
- Set up an account with an email marketing platform that works with your Weebly app.
- Create a list or audience that you want sign-ups to go to
- Create a page on your website with a form using the app
- In the settings for the form, set the form submissions to go to your new list that you have set up in your email platform (for example, SumoMe settings so that data from completed forms go to your 'free eBook' list in MailChimp
- Now set up the automation in your email marketing platform

We will now cover how to create the automation.

Creating Automation Flow Emails

We will now look at how to create automation in your email marketing platform.

Here are the steps to creating automation. The steps, and wording will vary depending on which platform you use.

Step 1: Preparation

Automation needs a trigger and an action. The trigger is to tell the platform or the process when to perform the action which is to send an email. You may for example, set it up so that when a new subscriber is added to a list (the trigger) then send an email straight away with a link to a Lead Generation Product (the action).

The first trigger is automatically created by a form builder app such as JotForm which we discussed earlier.

Before setting up any automation, a list or audience needs to be created to send the emails to. It's also recommended to plan out an outline of what the flow of emails will look like, including the wording for each email that goes out at each stage.

To help you plan your flow of emails, I suggest either writing out the flow of emails with a pen and paper or using a spreadsheet to write down the steps of each flow. With a pen and paper, you can be more visual, but a spreadsheet outline might look something like this:

Step 1: Intro email
Wait 2 days
Step 2: Send out follow-up email
... and so on.

To help you write the content for your emails, I highly recommend using DripScripts by visiting www.dripscripts.com.

DripScripts promises to help you "Write high-converting email sequences in record time" and from experience, it's pretty good! DripScripts has a series of proven templates that they know get results. In other words, they write the sequence of emails for you using highly effective wording - and you can quickly import the content into your chosen email marketing platform.

Naturally, it's not perfect so you will most likely need to make changes to your emails but it's a brilliant tool for generating inspiration, getting you started and saving you time.

I strongly recommend looking at their Welcome New Subscriber template which they have tested and is known to get results.

Step 2: Initial Setup

Once you have created a list and know what you will include in your sequence of emails, it's time to set up the automation and the process flow.

Click on Automation (or whatever the wording is in your email platform) and create an automation. Some platforms will present you with different automation options such as for dealing with shopping cart abandonment on eCommerce sites, date-based activities (which are great for sending a happy birthday email including a voucher if you own a restaurant) and much more. You might want to use one of those for your business but to keep it simple, we are going to run through setting up a standard automation.

The next step is to set up the triggers and actions.

Step 3: Triggers and Actions

Now you will see a workflow area which will be blank, and the screen might possibly show a prompt to set up your first action.

We won't go through all of the workflow here but let's look at the first 2 to get you started.

Click to create your first trigger and make sure it's set up to trigger an email immediately once a new subscriber is added to your chosen list. If you have several lists or audiences, make sure to select the one that you want to use in this campaign.

You don't want people who sign up for one thing to receive a series of emails that are completely irrelevant!

You will need to create or copy and paste the wording for your first email.

If you are copy and pasting from another source, make sure that any links are working. If you are using DripScripts to create your content, then make sure to follow the instructions that they provide.

Once you have created your trigger or action, you might need to click on Edit to make changes. If you are happy with the first trigger and action, move to the next step down in the flow.

For the next email, you will need to make sure there is a small pause before it goes out. You don't want emails 1 and 2 to go out at the same time when someone signs up, and when I say "pause", I mean a number of days, not a pause of 15-20 minutes (which is enough time for an English person like myself to grab an afternoon cup of tea).

If you are using Mailchimp, the next block or action is to create a delay. Click on the + symbol and create a delay of, for example, 48 hours. After that, click on the + symbol again and create your second email.

If you are using SendFox, then the delay settings are in each email block. In other words, once you have created the first email, click below that to add a second email rather than a delay. Within the boxed area for each email, you will see an option to delay that email by a set period.

I hope that makes sense. Each hosting platform has a slightly different way of presenting the flow of automated emails, but the important thing here is to make sure that you link it to the right email list and that there is a delay between each email.

Once this is done you have set up your first trigger. The flow will go something like this:

MailChimp receives an email address from your site which goes into your list
The first trigger is activated, and an email goes to the subscriber immediately
There is now a delay of 48 hours before the second email is sent to the subscriber

This is only an example, and you can set the number of days differently as well as add variation so that more emails are sent in the initial stages and the gap between emails are slightly longer later on.

An example might be where you are providing a 5-day challenge such as 'master LinkedIn with this 5-day challenge' or 'learn how to create a healthy routine with this 5-day challenge'. For this, you might send an email every day for 5 days and then a series of emails with gaps of 2-3 days instead of every day.

You can now add more emails to the flow. For the next sequence of emails, follow the steps above.

There are other elements you can have that allow you to send the subscriber in a different direction depending on their status. In MailChimp, this is using label and IF routines. For example, if a subscriber has the label 'purchased subscription' then send them this sequence of emails instead.

The ability to create multiple flows depending on the characteristics of the subscriber is enormously powerful, but it can easily be overcomplicated.

We aren't going to go through this in detail here but if you do decide to create various sequences them make sure to plan it out properly beforehand and try to keep it as simple as possible!

Once everything is set up how you would like it, activate the workflow.

With the email integration to your website in place and the email automation set up, you are good to go!

It's always important to test it properly to make sure it's working ok, as well as measure how effective it is.

It may be that the emails are too frequent, or there aren't enough call to actions in your emails to convert.

The great thing about automation is that you have now freed up time through automation to be able to measure and modify your process so that it's optimized to get you the best results.

Additional Email Marketing Tips

So far, we have gone through the essentials to making your email marketing highly effective, but there are always ways to make your email marketing even more effective.

We have worked through the process of setting up an email campaign including the critical elements to success such as the right wording, catchy headlines and avoiding spam folders. We have also set up an automation to save you time and to get better results.

This next section focused on activities that you can do to improve your campaign which is already running. Here are some additional tips that could make your results better still.

Integration with social media

Did you know that Twitter allows you to import your contacts so that you can follow them? If you want to get closer to your customers then visit the Settings section in Twitter, select Find Friends and import your contacts from Gmail or Outlook.

Twitter will retrieve the accounts it can find based on those email addresses and present you with a button to follow all of them immediately.

Facebook, LinkedIn, Pinterest and other great platforms also have similar functionality which means you can increase the interactions with your customers by using both email and social media together.

Research shows that the more contact or touch points you have with a prospect, the more likely they will trust you and therefore buy from you. If someone subscribes to your email campaign and they also see your posts in their social feed, then they are more likely to interact and engage with your brand.

If you sell to other businesses, then it's also good to interact with the posts from those businesses as well by liking, commenting or even sharing their posts.

Integrating email marketing activities with social media is a powerful way to build a base of loyal customers but always make sure that the activities you do are in line with privacy regulations such as GDPR and that the privacy of the individual is respected. Exporting data for example, from LinkedIn to use in other campaigns such as email marketing might be a breach of LinkedIn terms and conditions as well as being illegal.

Measure, test and improve

There's a saying *"if you always do what you've always done, you'll always get what you've always got."*. It's a bit tricky to say but put simply – if your marketing isn't working, and you aren't getting results then don't keep doing more of the same, ineffective activities!

Even if you are getting good results, could you do things even better? There is nearly always scope for improvement, even if you are getting great results.

Monitor the results you are getting and try things differently. This can include a number of things such as changing the time of day or day that you send emails out, whether your subject line includes a question or 'how to' sentence and even where you include the links in your copy.

Before and during an automation campaign test it thoroughly to make sure that it looks good on a mobile or tablet as well as desktop. Proofread the wording to make sure there aren't any grammar or spelling mistakes and review the content to see if you can make it easier to read and more effective (including increasing open rates and clicks on the call to action).

It's worth spending a little bit of extra time on this last point to see if you can add in any power words and to check that your call to actions are irresistible.

Over time, it's also worth monitoring the open rate as well as the clicks to see how they perform. It could be that a slight change of the subject might increase the open rate or changing the wording in the call to action dramatically increases the click rate.

Don't underestimate the power of good content!

Consider split testing

This is a feature that most email platforms offer and something I've kind of suggested in the last section. When you write a campaign, you can produce two versions and see what the difference is in results. This allows you to decide which wording is more effective for future campaigns.

It's best to make changes one step at a time. If you make lots of changes and the open rate or clicks in your emails go up, then it's hard to know what worked. When using split testing, pick an objective that you want to measure and then create two versions of the campaign.

A good objective to start with is to improve open rates. To do this, create two or more subject lines to see which email gets a higher open rate. Let's imagine that you provide advice on personal investments and you want to send an email with tops tips for retirement planning. You might come up with the following subject lines:

7 ways to plan successfully for your retirement
Want to know how to plan for retirement successfully?
How to plan for the best retirement

You can now use either 2 or all 3 subject lines and do some split testing.

If you have a targeted list of 10,000 members and decide to test out just the first 2 subject lines, then it's wise to test the two headlines out on a small sample first, say, 2,000 subscribers.

Once you know which one is best, you can then use that subject line for the remaining 8,000 subscribers.

The sample needs to be big enough to give you the results you want. Just sending the campaign out to 100 or 200 subscribers might not provide enough evidence to say which subject line is best. On the other hand, you don't want to test it on too many of the subscribers in your list, otherwise you won't have enough subscribers left for the main campaign!

Here's an example of how the above split testing scenario might work.

After sending out your campaign to 2,000 subscribers you find that the open rates are as follows:

7 ways to plan successfully for your retirement
Emails opened: 312 (31.2% open rate)

Want to know how to plan for retirement successfully?
Emails opened: 247 ((24.7% open rate)

From this, you can see that the first version clearly has a higher open rate, and while you can't guarantee that the open rate will be the same with the remaining 8,000 subscribers, you can feel much more confident that this wording is more effective.

If the same open rates applied to the remaining 8,000 subscribers, then 2,496 emails would be opened and read with the first version versus 1,976 for the second version.

A difference of 520 more readers!

That's quite a difference, and even if 1% of opens lead to a sale of $200, then that's an extra $1,000+ in sales! (1% of 520 being 5.2 customers spending $200 each…).

The above numbers are only examples, but you can apply your own formula to your own business, and you will quickly see how split testing can help you to achieve much more sales.

Consider the other parts of the sales process

Email marketing doesn't stand alone, and sometimes its success or failure can be impacted by the other parts of the sales process for your business.

If you are using advertising to drive potential customers to your website where they can sign up for a lead generation product, then the effectiveness of the campaign can depend on other factors such as:

- How cleverly written the ad is and how well it attracts your audience to want to visit your site
- Who you are targeting and how you are targeting them with the ads campaign
- The design of the landing page and how well it is enticing them to provide their email address
- How compelling the offer, itself is, and what value it adds to the website visitor

The above factors can be broken down into **advert**, **landing page** and **offer**.

A badly created Facebook advert, for example, that doesn't grab the attention of the prospect or targets the wrong people in the ad is likely to have low click throughs to the website.

It doesn't matter how good your landing page is or how brilliant your emails are that you will send out – if nobody signs up to it from the Ads campaign.

If the advert is optimized to get the best results, then the next area to consider is how effective the landing page is at enticing the visitor to take action. The landing page should consider elements such as:

- Social Proof (this product has been downloaded 10,000 times or has over 500 5-star reviews)
- A guarantee (this product is guaranteed to make a difference)
- Scarcity and/or a strong call to action (This offer ends in 2 hours. Claim your voucher now!)
- Being mobile friendly so that it's easy to use on a mobile phone
- An easy to fill in form that's not over-complicated

The more effective the landing page, the more subscribers you will get to your campaign.

There's a lot to consider with a landing page and if you would like to know more then you might be interested in my book **How to create a perfect landing page** (available on Amazon)

When measuring the results of an email marketing campaign, measure and review all elements of the campaign to get a better picture.

You might think that email marketing isn't getting results when in fact the problem lies with the website, the advert or something else.

An example I often see of this is where businesses don't have their website optimized for mobile. On a desktop, the Lead Generation campaign looks good and makes sense, but in reality, the campaign doesn't get the results it should because the majority of visitors to the website use their mobile phones.

When viewed on a mobile phone, the form might be difficult to fill in or the user can't read the text and simply gives up because it's too painful trying to find out more about the offer.

Perfect Email Marketing Recap

We've covered a lot in a relatively short amount of time and pages, but here is a list of key points from the book:

Email marketing is highly effective and will continue to be for many years to come. If you aren't using email marketing already then you should! (Unless you don't want to grow your sales – but then you probably wouldn't be reading this book!).

There are various ways email marketing can help with sales and marketing from up selling and generating repeat business to helping convince customers to make their first purchase.

First time buyers often require many contacts or touchpoints to build trust with your brand, and the best way to do this is to use email marketing with other channels such as social media and ads.

One of the best ways to generate leads and convert opportunities is by combining Lead Generation Products with email marketing.

Content in an email is critical to success. If you don't add value to the reader and you don't include a call to action then you will waste time, experience higher unsubscribes and not generate sales.

The subject in an email is NOT an afterthought. It's vital that it is attractive and appealing.

If the subject line doesn't convince the reader to open the email, they will never see what you have to say, no matter how great the content is inside!

Great subject lines entice the reader to open the email, great headlines and first paragraphs make the reader want to find out more.

Call to actions take the reader to the next level in the sales process.

Testing and checking what you have written before launching a campaign is important. Spending just an extra 5 or 10 minutes to make sure the emails make sense could make a huge difference in how effective your email campaign is.

Many people read emails on their mobile phone. Checking it is optimized for mobile is important.

There are always ways to improve a campaign, no matter how good it is!

Making minor changes and measuring the results is a good way to see how you can improve a campaign. So is the use of split testing.

Email automation can save hours, convert more enquiries and generate more sales. It takes effort setting it up but once it's done you will be glad!

Thanks! (And next steps)

A big thank you again for choosing this book. I hope you found it useful and valuable.

It's always great to learn how to do things better, but the only way to make it worthwhile is to implement what has been learnt, so I recommend spending some time now to plan out your next marketing campaign and to revisit the book throughout the implementation process to give you plenty of ideas and inspiration.

If you have any questions or would like me to review the content of an email campaign, then feel free to email me a test email from your email software. I would be happy to provide a free review with some basic feedback. You must let me know before you send the test email and mention that you purchased this book!

Send emails to:

darren@thinktwicemarketing.com

If you have enjoyed the book, please do leave a review on Amazon. It will really be appreciated and most importantly will help others immensely who might find the book of value.

We have covered a lot in this book, but we aren't quite finished yet!

At the back of the book is a list of tools and websites that you can use as part of your email marketing. I have also included some bonus offers.

Many thanks again, and I wish you all the best in your email marketing efforts!

To your success!

~ Darren

Bonus Offers

As a thank you for purchasing this book, I'm delighted to offer you extra materials to help you with your marketing, including a list of power words that you can use in your content and a range of templates that you can copy and paste into your email platform. I'm adding content all the time and it's all available by visiting the link below:

https://hi.switchy.io/emailmarketingoffer

The above link is an example of a landing page with an offer. Once you enter your email address you will get an email with links to the bonus materials. You will also receive a sequence of emails with tips and support that expand on the content in this book.

I recommend staying signed up to the automation that I've created so that you can benefit from the tips and advice, but of course, you can unsubscribe at any time.

If you leave a review for this book and email me a link to the review, then I would be delighted to provide you with a free 1-hour support session over the phone or a video call.

If this is of interest, just email the link for your book review. Email me at: darren@thinktwicemarketing.com and let me know when you are available for a chat (make sure to include any other links or materials that might be useful for the call, including links to landing pages etc).

Tools

With years of experience searching for the right tools, testing them out and seeing what works I have some good news! You don't need to spend quite so much time doing the same. Below is a list of solutions that can help you with your email marketing, split into various categories.

The list isn't exhaustive and there are new tools being launched all the time, but the information below will be a big help in getting you started!

Software is a dynamic fast-moving industry so you might also find that some of the apps have new features or have changed in pricing.

Creating Forms
SumoMe
WuFoo
JotForm
Form Stack
123 Contact Form
Cognito Form

Creating pop-ups
Wise Pops (www.wisepops.com)
SumoMe
Scroll Trigger Boxes for WordPress (www.wordpress.org/plugins/scroll-triggered-boxes)

Other WordPress plugins include: Hello Bar, Mango Buttons, WordPress Calls To Action and WP Pop-Up

Email Marketing Software
MailChimp
SendFox
Moosend
Constant Contact
Campaign Monitor
AWeber
Vertical Response

Other email software solutions include Emma (www.myemma.com), Mad Mimi, FeedBlitz, Inbox First, Klaviyo, Vero, Drip, MailerLite, WhatCounts, ConvertKit

Automated Integration Tools
These tools can be used to integrate two or more apps. They act as a bridge between them.
Zapier
IFTTT

Creating a free guide or eBook
Attract.io
Beacon (www.beacon.by)
Blurb
eBook Adaptations

Creating landing pages
Swipe Page (https://swipepages.com)
Lead Pages (https://leadpages.pxf.io/c/2512723/575865/5673)
Weebly (https://www.weebly.com)

Also see the list of fully functioning solutions below, including Click funnels.

Fully functioning powerful software solutions
HubSpot
Click funnels
New Zenler
Wishpond (focused specifically on landing page automation)
Kissmetrics
Infusionsoft
Ontraport
GetResponse
Pardot

Writing content for your email
Grammarly
DripScripts

My other books that might be of interest:
How to create a perfect landing page
Blogging for business
Psychology in Marketing and Sales

To see my full range of books, visit www.thinktwicemarketing.com/resources.

Thanks again and **don't forget to redeem your bonus materials for free!**

All the best with your email marketing.

Printed in Great Britain
by Amazon